GOING for the GOAL

TERRY HILL

BROADMAN PRESS
NASHVILLE, TENNESSEE

This book is dedicated to those men who give of themselves to serve as chaplains to the National Football League teams. Men like Dave Bratton, Scott Opplinger, Charlie Collins, Dave Wilson, and John Webber will never realize the full extent of their ministry here on this earth. Thank you for being obedient to God and for sharing that obedience with other men who so greatly influence our youth.

© Copyright 1990 ● Broadman Press
All rights reserved
4269-50

ISBN: 0-8054-6950-8
Dewey Decimal Classification: 248.4
Subject Heading: CHRISTIAN LIFE // ATHLETES - RELIGIOUS LIFE
Library of Congress Card Catalog Number: 90-30423
Printed in the United States of America

Unless otherwise stated, all Scripture quotations are from the King James Version of the Bible.

Scripture quotations marked NASB are from the *New American Standard Bible.* © The Lockman Foundation, 1960, 1962, 1963, 1968, 1971, 1972, 1973, 1975, 1977. Used by permission.

Thanks to the Fellowship of Christian Athletes for some of the material in chapter 12 about Jay Schroeder, which is reprinted from an article entitled "Passing Remarks."

Library of Congress Cataloging-in-Publication Data
Going for the Goal / [edited by] Terry Hill.
        p.   cm.
    ISBN 0-8054-6950-8
    1. Football players—United States—Biography. 2. Football
    players—United States—Religious life. I. Hill, Terry.
GV939.A1G65 1990
796.332'092'2   dc20
    [B]   90-30423
                                                              CIP

Contents

Acknowledgments

I would like to thank some young men who inspired me to invest my time writing this book: Terry II, Robbie III, Danny Boy, Lyle, Michael, and Jonathan. Because of them and other children of Christian parents, I have tried to provide positive Christian athletic role models for them to look up to.

I also thank each public relations office of these NFL teams, Vanderbilt University, and Bruce McLellan of *The Nashville Banner* for their cooperation in providing information and pictures.

And a big thank you must go to the players in the NFL who boldly stand and proclaim Jesus Christ as Savior and Lord in their daily lives, on and off the field. Their testimonies will have an effect that will be fully recognized only in eternity.

REGGIE WHITE, Defensive End, Philadelphia Eagles, 6'6"—285 lbs. (PHOTO COURTESY OF PHILADELPHIA EAGLES)

1
Reggie White
Defensive End
Philadelphia Eagles

"I wanted to be a minister and a pro football player."

A lot of people say I was crazy for withdrawing my name from the list to receive the award for "Lineman of the Year." I did it, and would gladly do it again as long as the event is sponsored by an alcoholic beverage company. What they stand for and what I stand for don't even come close to mixing.

I still received "Defensive Player of the Year" in 1987 and came close to being NFL "Player of the Year." Now you might say that was an incredible accomplishment for a little boy from Chattanooga who quit football once because he was afraid of getting hurt by the big boys. But when I was in junior high, I set a goal to be two things in this life: a minister and a football player. Now, I am one of the big boys, all 6'6" and 285 pounds of me.

I started playing organized football when I was ten. The Dixie Youth League folded, and I didn't play again until junior high. Man, those guys were big, so I quit because I didn't want to get hurt. I started back again a year later when I was a little bigger, and I did pretty good. I also liked basketball and made the All-City team in the ninth grade.

I went to an all-black church that had a white preacher named Rev. Ferguson. He really had a great impact on my life by the way he loved and treated the people in our church. He made me want the same Jesus he had. I mention Rev. Ferguson's name a lot because I hope he'll hear about me someday, and then I can thank him in person for his life and the example he set for me.

When I was about thirteen, a guy named Ed Christie, who was a student at Tennessee Temple College in Chattanooga, led me to invite Christ into my life. Rev. Ferguson planted the seed, and Ed Christie watered it. I immediately started sharing Christ. One of the first verses of Scripture I attempted to learn was misinterpreted by me as, "Thou shalt kill them that 'lease.' " Later I found out that *lease* was "lies,"so I went around school telling kids that I was going to have to kill them if they kept lying.

I started setting goals after I became a Christian, because I had read that "Where there is no vision [or goal], the people perish [or die]" (Prov. 29:18). During that time I set those two goals, and today I am—I hope—exactly what God and I wanted me to be. Of course, I'm not everything He wants, but I am really trying hard to be all He wants. Those goals didn't happen because Reggie White sat around and waited for them; they happened because I worked hard for them and because I tried to let Jesus control everything I did. Whenever the papers or television reporters interviewed me, I made sure I gave Jesus all the credit, because I knew how I got to where I was.

I graduated from Chattanooga High School where I had been an All-State basketball player and an All-American football player. I accepted a football scholarship to play for the University of Tennessee Volunteers (Vols). When I got there, I set the goal of becoming the Southeastern Conference "Player of the Year." This was a pretty high goal since no defensive player had received it since 1968 when Jake Scott of Georgia won it. Well, in 1983 I was the first defensive player to win Southeastern "Player of the Year" in fifteen years. I was the first Tennessee player to win it since Johnny Majors, my coach with the Vols, won it when he was an outstanding Vol player in the mid-1950s. When I started the 1983 season, I didn't expect anything less. My mind was set, and no one could tell me anything different.

A kid asked me how I got my strength on the football field: "Do you pray for it?" he asked.

I said, "Sure I do, but I know the only way God will give me maximum strength on the field is to get in the weight room and then out on the track. We can't ask God to give us something if we're not willing to work with all our might to receive the best."

Being "Defensive Player of the Year" and being named MVP in the Pro Bowl are great honors. But when I die, I don't want people to remember what Reggie White did in football: I want them to remember what Reggie White did as a man of God. I have a beautiful Christian wife, Sara, who challenges me to be all I should be as a Christian father and husband. More than anything, I want my children to want the same Jesus that is in their Mom and Dad.

HOWARD CROSS, Tight End, New York Giants, 6'5"—245 lbs.
(PHOTO COURTESY OF NEW YORK GIANTS)

2
Howard Cross
Tight End
New York Giants

"After a year of playing at Alabama, I went back to my old high school and shared my testimony."

My parents got a divorce when I was twelve, and my brother and sister went to live with my mother. I went with Dad who remarried a short time later, and then I gained a new little brother. I spent the rest of my younger years with my new family and adjusted pretty well.

I started playing football when I was five just because all the other kids were doing it. Your team and division were determined by your weight. I was always a pretty big fellow, so I always played with guys older than me until I was in middle school.

My favorite sport was basketball. "Dr. J.," the great Julius Erving, was my idol, and every time we went to the playground, I was Dr. J. Even in high school, my main game was basketball. I played football, but we were terrible. In our best year we went 4-6. Our last game in my junior year,

we were beaten 50-0! I couldn't believe that anyone would be interested in me as a football player.

At the end of the football season, a college coach
told me I could be a good football player. I almost
laughed at him because I thought basketball was
my game.

Then a short time later, I was warming up for
basketball practice when this same coach came
into the gym. I immediately thought he had
brought some basketball coaches with him, so I began to really put on a show.

After practice the coach approached me and re-
marked how good I was in basketball, and then he
said he thought I could be an even better football-
player. I was shocked! I had already decided that I
wasn't even going to play football my senior year,
but the coach talked me into it.

I had a pretty good senior year and graduated
from New Hope High School in New Hope, Alabama. I even accepted a full scholarship to play
football for the Crimson Tide of the University of
Alabama.

While at Bama, I was fortunate to receive several honors. As a freshman, I played tight end and
weighed only 210 pounds. I then started on a
weight training program that boosted me to my
present weight of 245 pounds. In my junior year, I
was All-Southeastern Conference "Player of the
Year," and I was best known as a good blocker.

Throughout my senior year, I continued to build
my blocking and receiving skills, and I was voted

to receive the Jacobs Trophy as the outstanding blocker in the SEC. I was privileged to play in the Senior Bowl and then was drafted in the sixth round by the New York Giants in 1989.

I grew up in church and was always there, whether I wanted to be or not. I joined the church when I was very young, but I don't think I really understood what being a Christian meant. A few years later, at church I personally invited Christ into my life, and I don't think I realized what had happened to me at that time.

I really began to grow while I was in high school. Christ in my life was causing me to be friends with everyone, good people and bad. I had something, and I wanted to share it, but I wasn't sure how to go about it.

When I got to Alabama, a friend named Ricky Thomas really helped me to get involved with the Fellowship of Christian Athletes. During this time I learned how to grow as a Christian and how to share my faith. Then one night, I decided to pray and tell God that I wanted to be sure I was a Christian just in case I hadn't known what I was doing when I was younger.

About a year and a half after I graduated from high school, I was invited back to my old school to speak. I asked the principal to call together the Leadership Club. I told them about how, when I was in school, we were going to make this the best school in the state: drug free, alcohol free, and the whole works. I told them I had learned the key to making all of this happen, and I would tell them all about it if they would come to hear me at an assembly the next day.

The next day I spoke to the elementary kids and the junior high kids, and then came the senior high kids. I proceeded to begin a speech that lasted almost a solid hour. I started out talking about my research on cocaine and other drugs including alcohol and tobacco. I then continued my speech right into my current relationship with God, and I explained who His Son, Jesus Christ, was and is. I then told them that my responsibility as a Christian was to tell them about Him. What they chose to do with Him was up to them.

One guy stood up and started clapping, and then the whole student body joined in. I don't know how many chose to receive Christ that day, but I did what I was supposed to do in the toughest place to do it—where people know us and our past.

I'm looking forward to a long career in the National Football League. However, if it ends tomorrow, I'm not worried because I know the One who holds tomorrow in His Hands, and He has promised to take care of you and me.

SCOTT CAMPBELL, Quarterback, Atlanta Falcons, 6'0"—195 lbs.
(PHOTO COURTESY OF ATLANTA FALCONS)

3
Scott Campbell
Quarterback
Atlanta Falcons

"When your dad's a football coach, you don't play hockey."

Football and athletics have been a part of my life since I was a small boy. My father was a football coach, and he encouraged me but never pushed me. He told me I would learn to love it or hate it. I loved it!

My family's influence on my life goes far beyond athletics. My dad coached at the college level, but he was known as a rowdy man and a heavy drinker. As a result, my mom and dad's relationship and our home life were very shaky. Then one night when I was about six years old, my dad asked Jesus Christ to come into his life and be his Lord and Savior. He began an incredible change, and through his influence, my mom also became a Christian.

Soon I was going to church every time the doors were open. I accepted Christ as my Savior, also, and nothing really eventful happened. However, I know He came into my life. I was a good kid, too, because that is how my parents raised me.

During junior and senior high school, I was picked on a lot because of my athletic ability, and I struggled with that. I really didn't grow much as a Christian during that time.

In high school, my team went 10-1 during my junior and senior years. I passed for 3,892 yards, 28 touchdowns, punted for a 35-yard average, and even kicked a 35-yard field goal. I also played on the baseball and basketball teams, and I went to the Pennsylvania state finals in the javelin throw.

I accepted a full scholarship and went off to Purdue University to play football. With the Boilermakers, I became the second leading passer in Big Ten history behind only teammate Mark Hermann. I passed for 516 yards against Ohio State, and I was MVP my senior year at Purdue.

Then I was drafted in the eleventh round by my home state Pittsburg Steelers as a backup to Mark Malone and David Woodley. Later, I was released from the Steelers.

I was attending a Falcons game on the way to a vacation in Hilton Head, South Carolina, and during the game, Falcon starter David Archer separated his shoulder. "Scott Campbell" was paged to the press box, and the next day I signed my Falcon contract and was activated. That sure was an unexpected turn of events.

During this time when the Steelers released me, I was brought to my hands and knees. I saw that football really didn't matter. Proverbs 3:5-6 says:

> Trust in the Lord with all your heart,
> And do not lean on your own understanding.
> In all your ways acknowledge Him,
> And He will make your paths straight (NASB).

I learned to trust the Lord. The key was to acknowledge Him in all my ways, and I hadn't been doing that. He promised to direct my paths, if I would take notice of Him in my paths.

I got serious about my Christianity during the interval between Pittsburg and Atlanta. As a result I noticed less pressure in my life. Some things just didn't matter like they used to.

In 1988 there was no pressure to make the team since I'd started most of the last year, and I had done pretty well through some difficult circumstances. I'd shown my value to the team. Then the unthinkable happened. One play, and my season—possibly my football career—was over. I had seriously injured my knee.

It's tough to make goals like "I want to be the starting quarterback," or "I want to throw for so many yards," because you just don't know what's in the future. You can't make goals like that.

My goal now is to do everything I can for God's glory. I want to try my best—100 percent—because that is what God wants. The knee injury gave me a great chance to affect others through the attitude God gave me. I hope they can see through me that God gives us hope, and our spirits don't have to remain crushed because of rough times.

How I do in football doesn't amount to a hill of beans compared to the fact that God is always in control. He knows what is going on, and He will take great care of His children.

JOE MORRIS, Running Back, New York Giants, 5'7"—195 lbs.
(Photo courtesy of New York Giants)

4
Joe Morris
Running Back
New York Giants

"Small in stature, huge in production . . ."

Having five brothers and sisters will teach anybody a whole lot about competition. Being "army brats," we moved around some, but I had great parents and a family whom I love and appreciate very much.

I was born and raised in Fort Bragg, North Carolina, but I moved to Massachusetts for my last two years of high school. My dad was a strong disciplinarian who believed in doing things right. He would give me a chore to do, and many times he would wake me up from my sleep to do it again and again until it was right. This discipline really carried over into my athletic career, and it has helped me tremendously.

I started playing football when I was in fourth grade, and when I moved to Massachusetts, they made good fun of my Southern drawl. Being short was always a detriment until I was given a chance to prove myself. I had to prove myself from the time I started playing in Peewee League games until the first day I walked on the practice field with the New York Giants.

I was chosen All-State at Ayer High School in Ayer, Massachusetts, and then accepted a full scholarship to attend a great school for running backs, Syracuse University. Because I was five feet, seven inches tall, many people said I should have gone to a small college, but I knew what I could do.

While at Syracuse I broke the all-time rushing records of Jim Brown, Larry Csonka, and Floyd Little by rushing for 4,229 yards in four seasons. I also set the one-game mark of 252 yards against Kansas, and I had twenty-one games with 100 yards or more. In my senior year, I was an All-American and played in the Senior Bowl, the East-West Shrine game, and the Blue-Gray game in Alabama.

My favorite memory of a game is the last game of my senior year at the Carrier Dome. I had hoped my parents could come and see me play, but they told me they couldn't. Then at the last minute, some friends talked my mom into coming with them, and she had to buy scalpers' tickets to see me play. We upset West Virginia that day, and the fans had us come out of the dressing room to take a bow. It was then I saw my mom and got to hug her. That was a great ending to my college career because my mom had always said I was too small to play football.

While I was in high school in Massachusetts, my mom also invited me to go with her to church. I respected her so much that I went mainly to please her. Calvary Baptist Church sent a bus out to the base where my dad was stationed, and we would ride it to church.

I remembered Mom telling me that going to Sunday School and church was going to reveal some areas in my life that my success in football could not cover up. After we had attended a few weeks, I went forward during a service and asked Jesus to come into my life, and then I was baptized. I thought that this was all there was, but it was kind of neat. That was the extent of my Christianity until I came to the Giants' Bible studies with our chaplain, Dave Bratton. I thought that persons became Christians, and then they just sort of cruised through life without having to do another thing. Boy, was I wrong!

I was drafted by the Giants in the second round, and now I have had a pretty successful professional career. I'm the all-time leading rusher in Giants history, and I have made the Pro-Bowl on two different occasions. Then we won the Super Bowl. That was really exciting!

I guess the person who most influenced my life on the Giants was George Martin. George sure did walk the walk of a Christian, and he made me want what he had. I was a Christian, but I didn't know anything about this personal walk with Christ. I went to all the chapels we had before our games, but still I didn't have this personal walk with Christ.

Then I fell in love with a beautiful lady, and we wanted to get married. I went to our team chaplain, and Dave said he didn't have a problem marrying us, but he did have a problem marrying a couple in which one or both were not Christians. Through our counseling with Dave, Linda became a Christian, and I learned how to begin my relationship with Christ on a daily basis.

Dave then began a one-on-one discipleship program that helped me learn to have a daily quiet time with the Lord and how to grow spiritually into the man God wants me to be. The best thing I know now is that Joe Morris cannot be in control of my life, but God has to be, or I am nothing.

If a kid came up to me and told me he wanted to play pro football and wanted to know what he could do to help himself, I'd say this:

You have to have the right priorities. You must have God first, your family second, and then everything else will fall into place. The average professional life of a football player is 2.1 years. Even if you play ten years, you've still got a lot of life after football.

The reason you go to school is not to play football but to get an education so you can live. If you put football first, you will have nothing left when football is over. Football can be taken away at anytime, but your relationship with Christ can't!

BOB BREUNIG, Former Middle Linebacker, Dallas Cowboys, 6'2"—225 lbs. (PHOTO COURTESY OF DALLAS COWBOYS)

5
Bob Breunig
Middle Linebacker
Dallas Cowboys

"The privilege of playing in several Super Bowls and Pro Bowl is very gratifying, but . . ."

While I was playing football at Alhambra High School in Phoenix, Arizona, I remember that an assistant coach by the name of Bill Saloni taught me the fundamentals of hard work—to keep striving and to constantly give it my best. I've never forgotten the lesson he taught me about football, especially to work hard at what I was doing.

Those lessons I learned from Coach Saloni have followed me throughout my years at Arizona State and into my professional career with the Cowboys in Dallas.

As a young rookie, fresh out of college, I broke my foot in a very crucial game, and I had to be sidelined for several weeks. I worried about how long it would take the foot to heal before I could be back on the line. I wondered if I would be put on the injured reserve list and miss my first Sugar Bowl game. For four weeks, those fears haunted me.

Now, as I look back at those difficult weeks, I realize that God was using this valuable time for spiritual growth. My decision to accept Christ into my life during my senior year at Arizona State was beginning to take on new meaning. I was learning patience and perseverance in a different light. Within four weeks, I was able to get back on the playing field, playing harder than ever before, and I helped my team win a Super Bowl berth. Although I didn't want to miss any of the games in my rookie year, I'm glad now that God put me aside to learn many things I might have missed if I had continued to play. Besides many honors and records at Arizona State, two great events took place in my life while there. I met my wife-to-be, Mary Matthews, during my junior year, and I was introduced to a personal relationship with Jesus Christ by three particular persons who influenced me greatly.

These three persons were Roger Gehring, a staff worker for a local Christian organization; a professor by the name of Bill Broody; and the parents of Mary's best friend, Phil and Thelma Steinberg of Los Angeles.

Roger's outgoing, happy personality, Professor Broody's practical answers to biblical principles, and the Steinbergs's radiant Christian life-style caused me to want what they had. I soon learned that the only way I could have these things was through a personal relationship with Christ. I must admit that I focused my attention on the created things and not the Creator. Only when I began to focus my life on Christ did I find the satisfaction I longed for. Winning trophies and honors just didn't cut it. I wanted more out of life.

One of the passages in the Bible which I love to quote when speaking before high school or college assemblies is found in Romans 12:1-2:

> I beseech you therefore, brethren, by the mercies of God, that ye present your bodies a living sacrifice, holy, acceptable unto God, which is your reasonable service. And be not conformed to this world: but be ye transformed by the renewing of your mind, that ye may prove what is that good, and acceptable, and perfect, will of God.

I have dedicated myself to the glory of God. I know that it takes a lot of hard work to be successful in any endeavor, as well as in the Christian life. I want Him to have any glory that may come from my life. It's easy to be pressed into the mold that the world offers, but I want to be what God would have me be. I am still in the growing process, and I will continue to work hard to achieve spiritual maturity.

My present goals are to live every day doing my best and to contribute as much as I can of my God-given talents to my team. Someday, I would like to look back and say that I gave it everything that I had.

The privilege of playing in several Super Bowl and Pro Bowl games is very gratifying to me, but nothing compares with knowing Jesus Christ as my personal Savior and Lord. All other things will pass away while my relationship with Him will last throughout eternity.

*After a super career Bob Breunig retired from the Cowboys.

MICHAEL HARPER, Wide Receiver, New York Jets, 5'11"—180 lbs. (PHOTO COURTESY OF NEW YORK JETS)

6
Michael Harper
Wide Receiver
New York Jets

"I carried the ball on the famous 'phantom touchdown' to beat Notre Dame on national television."

Kansas City, Missouri, is an excellent place for bringing up a family. It is just big enough to have everything you need, plus the traditional values you want to have your children grow up around. I was born and raised there, and I am very thankful for my parents. I'm still very close to my two sisters, even though they think I was a little spoiled being my mother's only boy!

We were a good, old Baptist church-going family. Sunday morning was always church, nothing else. My mother gave us no choice in this matter, even when we thought we were old enough to make our own decisions. Most of my relatives also lived in the Kansas City area; they attended church and provided an excellent family structure for me.

My family really instilled in me some outstanding work ethics. If I wanted an ice cream cone, I usually got one, but only after performing some task to let me know that nothing comes free. My Uncle Calvin and Uncle Benny and Uncle Paul, Jr., were very tough on me when it came to earning money. Then I didn't like their ideas all the time, but now I am thankful they were tough on me.

When I was in the sixth grade, my uncle was a coach for the Thirty-Ninth Street Boys Club in Kansas City, and he encouraged me to come out. I was small for my age, but I was real fast, so naturally I became a running back. My uncles bet with each other that I couldn't run around the block in two minutes. I loved that, and I would run like crazy. When I would beat the time, they would tell me that I couldn't do it again. Of course, I would give it my best shot each time. I sure got a lot of practice running.

I started playing regularly at Erving Junior High School in the Hickman Hills area. I didn't start much, but they said I certainly was fast. Then while a sophomore at Hickman Hills High School, I got to play tailback on the varsity team. They would always bring me in on one play called 42 Tackle Trap. What was so incredible is that whenever I ran that play, it would almost always be for a touchdown. Of course, we ran it only once or twice a game, so my playing time was limited.

I started at tailback during my junior year, and I had an excellent senior season with many awards. I was considered a "blue-chip" college prospect. Finally, I decided to attend the University of Southern California for my college football career and education.

When I got to USC, the other tailbacks were Charles White and Marcus Allen. If that wasn't overwhelming enough, every player there had been a "blue chipper" in high school. So the competition was intense, to say the least.

The most outstanding play I took part in was against Notre Dame in 1983. That was Coach John Robinson's last game at USC. It has been labeled the famous "Phantom Touchdown." We were behind on the scoreboard, and we had the ball on the two-yard line with just a couple of minutes left in the game. They called my number to run the ball, so I took the hand off and dove over the line into the end zone. When I hit the ground, I realized to my horror that I didn't have the ball. I immediately looked up at the referee and saw his hands lifted over his head signaling a touchdown.

Boy, was I relieved, until I saw the ball back on the two yard-line. Instant replay showed that I had lost the ball before I crossed the goal. By the way, we won the game on that touchdown, and Notre Dame probably lost the National Championship as a result. Guess who got it for "Player of the Game"?

I was drafted in the eleventh round by the Los Angeles Rams. I was cut three times and released from Calgary of the Canadian Football League before signing as a free agent with the Jets in 1986. I ran a kickoff back 97 yards for a touchdown against Cincinnati in the preseason. That is probably what convinced the Jets to sign me. As a matter of fact, I was the only player out of all the free agents and draft choices to make the team. I know that was of the Lord!

I asked Christ to come into my life when I was seven years old at church. However, I really didn't live in a day-to-day relationship with Christ until my sophomore year at USC when I rededicated my life. Three sisters at USC got me involved at the New Hope Baptist Church where I was challenged to advance past my salvation experience into daily fellowship through Bible study and prayer. I got involved with the Navigators, a Christian discipleship organization, and helped them get our Bible studies into the dorms.

You know, nothing in life has any guarantees. Whether we're playing football or trying to get an education, we need to do it for the right purpose. That purpose must be the Person of Jesus Christ. He's the only guarantee we can really have in this life (or the life to come). Don't live your life looking forward to the next touchdown or the roar of the crowd. When that happens, it is over instantly, and then it's gone. Don't perform for anybody or anything else without performing first for the One who will last—Jesus Christ!

STEVE LARGENT, Former Wide Receiver, Seattle Seahawks, 5'11"—185 lbs. (PHOTO COURTESY OF SEATTLE SEAHAWKS)

7
Steve Largent
Wide Receiver
Seattle Seahawks

"I wasn't fast enough to be a good receiver."

Not being blessed with great speed or good jumping ability, I have always had to rely on quick moves and sure hands to succeed in the National Football League. After several playoff games and Pro Bowls, I know that football can never take the place of what Jesus Christ means in my life.

During my sophomore year at Tulsa University, I made an incredible discovery that changed my life. I had always believed in God, but I had never realized that I could have a personal relationship with Him. Our family had a little church background, and we always believed in having very high morals.

Then a friend asked me to go to some Christian organization on campus, and I went just to be with my teammates. That was the first time I had ever heard of knowing God personally.

A few weeks later, I went to a revival meeting at a local church in Tulsa, and I heard the gospel presented clearly and distinctly. That night I accepted Jesus Christ into my life, and things have never been the same since.

The next few years of college football were very exciting as I received many honors. During my first two years, I had caught only 33 passes for 501 yards and four touchdowns. But my last two years, I had made 103 catches for 1,884 yards and 28 touchdowns. I led the nation in touchdown catches with 14 each of my last two years.

I don't believe that accepting Christ has increased my athletic ability, but since I became a Christian, I know that He has given me confidence and peace, before, during, and after each game.

I was drafted by the Houston Oilers in the fourth round of the 1976 college draft. Then during the preseason, I was traded to the Seahawks where I have been ever since. I have started every game for the Seahawks except for those when I was injured. I have been fortunate to hold just about every receiving record that my team has.

I've been an All-Pro just about every year I've played, and I was named "Most Valuable Player" at the 1978 Pro Bowl in Los Angeles. One thing I try to remember is that I don't think Christ is always interested in the score. I really believe He is most interested in my performing to my full capacity. That's why I always try to give 100 percent on every down. Actually, I want to be a winner in Christ's eyes. If I can please Him, I'll be completely satisfied.

I really enjoy speaking to young aspiring athletes. I didn't become a Christian until I was twenty years old. I sure would have liked to have known Him when I was younger. That's what I would tell any young person who wants to be a better athlete: get Christ in your life, and then you'll have the confidence and assurance to be the best athlete you can possibly be!

*Having set nearly every pass-receiving record in the history of the NFL, Steve Largent retired at the end of the 1989 season.

FREEMAN McNEIL, Running Back, New York Jets, 6'2"—215 lbs.
(PHOTO COURTESY OF NEW YORK JETS)

8
Freeman McNeil
Running Back
New York Jets

"My mom gave me something that no one can ever take away."

I am one of the few babies of my generation to have been born in a house attended by a midwife instead a doctor in a hospital. Being born at home kind of set in motion a life-style of being close to my mother and the rest of my family that has lasted until now.

I cannot remember the first time I went to church, for Mom started taking me as soon as I was old enough to go. She just would not have had it any other way. As long as I was living in her house, I went to church. There were many times I didn't want to go, but now I am glad Mom did not give me any choice. Coming to know Christ as my Savior happened at an early age because of my mother's influence. I am so thankful that I didn't find Christ as a last resort to a major problem like so many other people do.

Believe it or not, I didn't start playing football

until I was fifteen years old when my mom and my stepfather moved to Carson, California. I just never was interested in football until then. With the encouragement of my brother, and an old photograph, I began playing football. I saw a picture of my dad, who had died when I was six, in his high-school football uniform. He wore #22. So, since I was Freeman McNeil, III, and the fourth Freeman in succession, I started wearing #24, the same number I had in high school, college, and the pros.

I had a very successful high-school career, and I was named Los Angeles City Player of the Year as a senior in 1976. I ran the ball for 1,343 yards with an 8.1 yards per carry average. We had an excellent team that helped me to score twenty-seven touchdowns that season. After graduation, I accepted a full scholarship to play for the UCLA Bruins and stay close to home.

While at UCLA, I was fortunate enough to set team records for yards in a season (1,396 in 1979) and most yards in a career (3,195). I made first-team All-American in my senior year with a 5.7 yards per carry average, and I finished seventh in total rushing in the NCAA. I ran for more than 100 yards in seventeen games while in college. My college career was highlighted when I caught a deflected pass against the USC Trojans and ran 58 yards for a touchdown and a 20-17 win.

I was a first-round draft choice by the New York Jets in 1981, the highest pick by the Jets other than Joe Namath and Johnny "Lam" Jones. I started six games during my rookie year, but I didn't really fit in consistently as a starter until the next year.

Last year I started all sixteen games at running back for the first time in my pro career. I was very blessed not to have gotten seriously injured during the whole season. I became the Jets' all-time leading rusher and finished seventh in the AFC in rushing. I am now the eighteenth all-time leading rusher in the NFL, and I need only 1,803 yards to move up to the number ten spot. I have also averaged more than 4.0 yards per carry all eight years of my NFL career, the longest streak among current NFL running backs. I also hold the team mark with twenty-six 100-yard rushing games in the regular season and three more during the play-offs.

There is no doubt in my mind who most influenced my life, athletically or otherwise—Mom. She gave me the knowledge of God. And that knowledge was not just a head knowledge but an everyday, good-time and bad-time working knowledge of God. I know without that solid basis, I would never have been anything. I get emotional and start to shed a few tears every time I think about it.

Some people inherit money, fame, or other things from their parents. I inherited something from my mother that can never be taken away: the knowledge of what God can do in your life through His Son: Jesus Christ.

Kids need to concentrate on where they are right now in their lives. What are you doing right now? For example: if you are in school, study so you can get the best education possible. Football or any athletics must be secondary. You must be fully prepared mentally before you can be fully prepared physically. And that's a fact!

JIMMY WILLIAMS, Linebacker, Detroit Lions, 6'3"—230 lbs. (PHOTO COURTESY OF DETROIT LIONS)

9
Jimmy Williams
Linebacker
Detroit Lions

"I didn't get a single college scholarship offer."

My dad owned several clothing stores in the Washington D.C. area, and every day after school, my brother and I had to work cleaning those stores. To be honest about starting to play football, we began playing to get out of working at the stores.

My brother, Toby, and I played football at a predominantly basketball school. Woodrow Wilson High School in Washington, D.C., was known for its great basketball teams. So football was hardly even noticed. Well, we were not that great as players either, and as a result, not one college offered us a scholarship. But we still wanted to play college football.

My dad was a pretty smart guy and told us to write a letter to several college recruiters telling about ourselves in hopes of getting a scholarship to one of their schools. We wrote the letter and sent it to at least a thousand colleges. Then the letters of rejection started coming in.

However, the University of Nebraska sent a letter that was very interesting about enrolling at the university and becoming a "walk-on" on the football team. This meant we had no guarantees of a scholarship, but if we made the team, we would then receive a scholarship. Then they followed the letter up with a phone call and a recruiting trip. Since that was the only offer, it was better than nothing. We accepted and went off to Lincoln, Nebraska, to become Cornhuskers under Coach Tom Osborne.

We couldn't believe how big the 78,000-seat stadium was. Then, there was the equipment we received as walk-ons. Because we were not the scholarship players, we were in back of the line to receive equipment, and it sure wasn't the best. This whole situation pushed me out of my comfort zone and forced me to work even harder to make the team.

After I received my first pair of football cleats, I noticed all the other players had brand-new shoes. My shoes were supposed to be white, but instead they were a deep, ugly gray. I asked why I didn't have the same new shoes as most of the other players, and the equipment manager told me I was a walk-on: I could take the shoes or leave them. I took those oversized, used shoes and walked back to my locker. I know everyone saw me, and many were laughing at me. It was a real humbling experience.

I practiced in those shoes, and I would take them home at night and glue them back together. I wore those shoes until I became a starter. Those shoes also forced me to play in tennis shoes a lot. As a matter of fact, when I did become a starter and was offered new shoes, I couldn't wear them on our turf grass because I was so used to playing in tennis shoes. I still play in tennis shoes today as a starter in the NFL.

I progressed through the ranks—from walk-on to starter and, finally, team captain my senior year. I also was an All-American, and I was drafted in the first round of the 1982 draft by the Detroit Lions. That was quite a turnaround for a guy who had to beg for a scholarship and practice in some used shoes!

Being a first-round draft choice in the NFL after having a great college career shot my ego about as big as any man's can get. I was an NFL linebacker, and I tried my best to live up to my role as a mean and tough guy that was ready to fight at the drop of a hat.

During my fourth year, I began to feel real lonely. I just couldn't understand how a professional football player living on top of the world in money and fame could feel lonely. I was talking with my mother, and she could sense the same thing I was feeling. After listening to me talk about all my accolades as a team captain and defensive MVP that year, she spoke up.

She told me that no matter how famous I got,

there was an area in my life that only God could fill. There's nothing else in the world that can ever fill that void. Well, that just blew me away because I had built my whole life on doing and being just what I was. Now my mom was saying that was not ever going to be enough. I shook that off as just being my mom, but my loneliness just got worse.

At that time, I was dating the lady who is now my wife, and she was a Christian, but I had told her that was her thing and not mine. Then one day, after we married, her sister was visiting us, and she asked how long it had been since we had been to church. I looked at Chris, and I could see the hurt in her eyes because it had been a long time, and the main reason was me. So, being the macho man I was, I told her I would take care of that, and we would go to church if it would make her happy.

The next Sunday we ended up at the wrong church, but we went in anyway. They say that every sermon has someone's name on it. The sermon that morning seemed like somebody had called the preacher and told him Jimmy Williams was coming. Every point of that sermon hit me to the core.

We left church, and I was mad as could be. I told Chris I would never go back to that church again. Well, the Holy Spirit started working on me, and I ended up going back a few weeks later, and eventually, I gave my life to Christ in a church service that summer.

Then I started attending chapel services with

the Lions and their chaplain: Dave Wilson. I got involved in Bible study with my wife and the other players and their wives, and I really started growing spiritually.

One of the most important things I have learned is that what you give will grow, and what you keep, you will eventually lose. When God gives you something, give it away, and you will get back so much more.

The Lions have not won as many games as we would have liked, but we have won many personal victories that will last a lot longer than professional football. Remember, the race is not given to the swift or the strong, but to those that endure and keep on going. I serve a mighty God, and you can serve Him, too!

MIKE SINGLETARY, Linebacker, Chicago Bears, 6'0"—228 lbs.
(PHOTO COURTESY OF CHICAGO BEARS)

10
Mike Singletary
Linebacker
Chicago Bears

"There's plenty more to do after winning a Super Bowl."

After winning Super XX in 1985, one might have said, "What else is there to do?" For me: plenty.

As a child I was pretty sickly, and the doctor told my parents I would probably never be an average little boy, much less a professional athlete. I had just about every disease a child could have. To make things worse, I was the youngest of ten children, so nothing ever came easily.

I grew out of the sicknesses and became a more-than-average, mean thirteen-year old. I was drifting in and out of trouble until, finally, I knew I had to make a decision about which way I was going to turn my life. During this time, my closest brother died, and my parents got a divorce. At a church service, I decided to let Christ into my heart and see if He could make a difference.

When I made that decision, I really didn't know what I had done. I really excelled in football and accepted a scholarship to Baylor University. Man, was college different from my days at Worthing High School in Houston! I made a pretty good adjustment to college life mainly because I had an outstanding Christian coach in Grant Teaff.

He was the type of man that didn't talk much about his faith because he didn't have to. By his actions on and off the field, we knew this man was a solid Christian we could always trust.

I had a pretty good college career at Baylor. I was a consensus All-American and the Southwest Conference "Player of the Year" in 1979 and 1980. I averaged fifteeen tackles a game and set a school record with 232 tackles in one season—in 1979. I was a finalist in the 1980 Lombardi Trophy for "Lineman of the Year," and I played in the Hula and Japan bowls my senior year.

While at Baylor, I really began to search and try to find out what being a Christian was all about. I saw several guys who said they were Christians but also had no problem getting drunk or high on drugs occasionally. That just didn't seem right to me. So I decided to read the Bible and see what it had to say. I read it all the way through, and I was amazed. I realized there was only one Word and only one God.

I was afraid that I might die, and, when asked why I should be let into heaven, I might have to alibi that a certain minister or famous Christian said I could. Now, I am a Christian and know I am going to heaven because I have done what the

Bible, God's Word, says I have to do.

The Bears selected me in the second round of the 1981 draft as the thirty-eighth player overall. It took me a couple of years in the pros to get adjusted. I was All-Pro in 1983, 1984, 1985, 1986, 1987, 1988, and 1989. In 1985 I was "Defensive Player of the Year." My nephew has asked me several times to help him so he can become a pro player like me. I tell him the same thing I would tell any young person who wants to be a good football player: put your education first. If you don't, you will never be the best player you can be. If you can't think straight off the field, there is no way you will think straight on the field during a game. Then you must make a commitment to doing your very best at everything you attempt to do. Work on and off the field. Practice, practice, and then practice some more. Learn the basics from the best available teacher. Then perfect what you have learned.

When you start playing, learn several positions and always listen to your coach. Most of all, be honest: admit it when you don't know what's going on. Don't be afraid to ask your coach anything.

You know, being a Christian is the most important thing in my life. But I don't have to yell and grab people to tell them where my faith is. They should be able to look at my life and my family and see something different. Remember the old saying, "Actions speak a whole lot louder than words."

DOUG COSBIE, Former Tight End, Dallas Cowboys, Denver Broncos, 6'6"—242 lbs. (PHOTO COURTESY OF DALLAS COWBOYS)

11
Doug Cosbie
Denver Broncos
Tight End

"I caught the go-ahead touchdown in the playoffs only to see Montana hit Clark to advance to the Super Bowl."

I grew up in Northern California and was always an avid San Francisco Forty-Niners fan. When I was ten, we moved to Mountain View where we lived until I went off to college. It was fantastic to catch a touchdown pass from Danny White that put us ahead of the Forty-Niners with six minutes left in the game at Candlestick Park. Then my heart sank as Joe Montana hit Dwight Clark for the winning touchdown with nothing left on the clock.

But that's football. Sometimes we have to remind ourselves that it's just a game!

I think I really became interested in athletics by watching my older brother, Danny, who was six years older than me, play everything. I started playing Pop Warner football when I was ten years old. I played football at Saint Francis High School in Mountain View under a great coach named

Mike Caldagno. He is still the coach there today. His first year of coaching was in my junior year, and we went 3-7. Then in my senior year we were 10-3 and went to the Central Coast sectional play-offs. To go from a tradition of losing to start a tradition of winning was very exciting.

I played football, basketball, and track at Saint Francis. I made the All-League team and played in the county All-Star game in football.

I was recruited by five or six schools, but I chose to go to a school near Boston called Holy Cross College. I went there and didn't like it much, so I transferred to Santa Clara where I played out my college career. In my senior year, I was the team captain and was voted MVP.

I wasn't an outstanding football player, but evidently I was good enough to be drafted by the Dallas Cowboys in the third round of the 1979 Draft.

I played backup to Billy Joe Dupree at tight end for a few years before getting to play regularly. I caught enough passes to pass Billy Joe in 1987, and became the all-time leading pass receiver among tight ends at Dallas. I'm also ranked fifth among all receivers on the Cowboys.

I really appreciate former Coach Tom Landry for having patience with me and my abilities. He easily could have let me go early in my career. I'm sure glad he saw my potential when others probably didn't.

I was fortunate to have played in three Pro Bowls in my career, and I was also voted the Cowboys' "Man of the Year" in 1984, an honor that recognizes the National Football League's top-citizen athletes. I've also been active in forming a youth-and-family growth center for troubled adolescents in the Dallas area.

I always had a head knowledge of who Jesus Christ was, but I had never invited Him to become a part of my personal life. It was at a chapel service before a game in 1980 that I invited Jesus Christ to come into my life and take control.

Since that time, through Bible study and chapel services, I've learned a lot about how to live the Christian life. It's kind of like watching your favorite team play a game. They get ahead, and you are really excited. Then they get behind, and you feel real bad. They start coming back and get real close at halftime. Then in the second half, they get behind again. This goes on and on until the game is over. This is what not being a Christian is like.

When you are a Christian, it's like watching the game on videotape. You know how it's going to end, so you don't get too worried about everything that happens in between. What an incredible sense of security we have as Christians!

I'll never forget what a friend of mine said that influenced my football playing as well as the rest of my life. He said, "Play football as though the outcome was completely up to you. Then pray to Jesus Christ as though the outcome was completely up to Him."

I think that's the best advice I have ever been

given. Do all that God has given you the ability to do. Then leave everything else up to Him and His will for your life.

After a distinguished career, Doug Cosbie retired from the Cowboys at the end of the 1988 season.

JAY SCHROEDER, Quarterback, Los Angeles Raiders, 6'4"—215 lbs. (PHOTO COURTESY OF LOS ANGELES RAIDERS)

12
Jay Schroeder
Quarterback
Los Angeles Raiders

"After four years in the minor leagues, I was batting .213, and I couldn't hit a slider."

It was November 19, 1985, and we were playing the New York Giants on ABC-TV's "Monday Night Football." With the score tied 7-7 in the second quarter, the great Joe Theismann went down with an injury that eventually ended his career. I was the backup quarterback, and after a long time-out, I was reluctantly put into the game. I say *reluctantly* because one of our coaches exclaimed, "Now what do we do?" Believe it or not, I really wasn't that nervous. Some people can't understand that. I knew I could perform, but most of all I knew whatever happened was going to be in God's hands, win or lose.

What really puzzles reporters is how I got to the NFL. After all, I had started only one game in my entire college career at UCLA. That's a little misleading, however, because I was at UCLA only two years before I decided I would have a better career in professional baseball.

After my sophomore year, I signed to play with the Toronto Blue Jays and was sent to Florence, South Carolina, the home of their Class A team. I really felt lost with my parents and fiancee, Debbie (now my wife), back in California. I saw many of my teammates doing things I thought were wrong, but I wasn't sure of what was right.

Then I talked to a man with Baseball Chapel about these questions, and he pointed me to a relationship with Jesus Christ. I listened to the message of Christ for several months, and then one night alone in my apartment, I invited Him to come into my life and take control.

Once I started praying and getting into His Word, the correct answers just kept coming. I finally let God guide me in the steps He wanted me to take with my life.

After four years in the minor leagues, I was batting .213, and I couldn't hit a slider. I had a great throwing arm, but I finally realized baseball was not my game. So in 1985, I made myself available for the NFL draft. To my unbelief, I was chosen by the Redskins in the third round and made the team as the backup to Theismann.

Coach Gibbs has a policy of giving most of the practice to the starting quarterback, so before that Monday night game, I had rarely taken snaps from the first-team center. When I went into that game, I had to draw strength from past experiences and, most of all, from God who was in control no matter what happened. Try to think of the best possible ending to that night on national television, and what happened to me was even better. On the first pass I hit wide receiver Art Monk for 44 yards. I ended up going 13-for-20 for 221 yards, and best of all, we beat the Giants 23-21.

The rest of that season went pretty well, too, as I completed 53.6 percent of my passes, and we won four of the five remaining games. Against Pittsburg I played my first complete game since high school.

In 1986, I was fortunate to become one of only eight quarterbacks in the history of the NFL to throw for more than 4,000 yards. I also made the Pro Bowl team and got to play in Hawaii.

I know my career could end at any time by an injury or by my not performing well. After my experience in baseball and football, I have learned not to get too excited or too depressed about my performance. I just have to remember the sun's going to come up tomorrow, and I'll have another chance to prove myself. Besides, my relationship with Christ, my family, and the church have given me more than professional football ever will.

*In 1988, Jay Schroeder was traded to the Los Angeles Raiders where he now plays.

WAYNE RADLOFF, Center, Atlanta Falcons, 6'5"—277 lbs.; Quar-terback Bob Holly behind him (PHOTO COURTESY OF ATLANTA FALCONS)

13
Wayne Radloff
Center
Atlanta Falcons

"They told me I was too little to play football."

England is not known for its American football. Being in an Air Force family stationed in England, I couldn't even try out for the team until the eighth grade. They said I was too small and too slow.

I guess I was a late bloomer, but my size and speed caught up with me about the tenth grade after we moved back to the States to Winter Park, Florida. In high school I realized that playing college ball was a real possibility.

I had a good senior year and was offered a scholarship to be a Georgia Bulldog under coach Vince Dooley. While at Georgia, a friend shared what a relationship with Christ was all about. I considered myself a Christian, but I didn't know God Himself. I rejected this personal relationship—knowing I ought to receive it—but seeming not to have a good reason to accept it.

During my Bulldog career, we won three Southeastern Conference Championships and one National Championship in 1980. We also had a decent running back named Herschel Walker. In my senior year, I made the All-SEC team and felt I had the world by the tail.

I snubbed the NFL and signed a good contract with the new World Football League and went to play for the Michigan Panthers. I really thought I was the model of success and would be the happiest person in the world. I had a lot of money and a very reliable girlfriend back home, but about two weeks later, my world came crashing down.

I had been lying to my girlfriend, who is now my wife, Garland. I was doing a lot of things that were flat wrong when she came to see me for a weekend. She found out about everything and left me. Two weeks later I told her that I had changed and convinced her to come and see me again. She came and found nothing but a bunch of new lies.

At the same time I had a back injury, and my career was in real doubt. I finally realized that football might not last forever. Now my girlfriend, and practically fiancee, was leaving me. I didn't know which way to turn.

Right before Garland got on the airplane, she turned and said she wasn't leaving without telling me something first. I couldn't figure out what was going on. We got back into the car and started driving. She began sharing with me what it meant to be a Christian. I knew what she was talking about, but I didn't know how to accept Jesus into my life.

We stopped in a small drug-store parking lot, and she prayed with me as I accepted Christ into my life. For me it was something that made sense right away. I felt myself wanting to change, and I felt the need to change.

After we finished praying, I was so excited, I wanted to tell someone. I went into the drug store and called Garland's parents, who were Christians, and explained to them, with tears in my eyes, what had just happened to me.

On the playing field, I am supposed to be a tough guy ready to knock another guy's block off. But since that night, I go onto the field to play to the best of my ability for Jesus. That's why He gave me the ability to play football: He knew I was going to become a Christian and that His purpose in my life was going to glorify His name.

JEFF RUTLEDGE, Quarterback, New York Giants, 6'1"—195 lbs.
(PHOTO COURTESY OF NEW YORK GIANTS)

14
Jeff Rutledge
Quarterback
New York Giants

"War Eagle or Roll Tide?"

Growing up in a football-crazy town like Birmingham, Alabama, you had only one thing on your mind: Roll Tide or War Eagle. Of course that means if you wanted to play college football, you had to choose between Auburn University or the University of Alabama. Actually, I had to make a hard decision between Alabama and the Louisiana State University Tigers.

I had a great time growing up in a strong Christian family. My parents were very strict in their discipline which, at the time, I didn't like. However, as I got older and left home, I realized how important it was and will be for my own children.

Dad was a professional baseball player for the Chicago Cubs for a while, and he really pushed me hard to excel in athletics. My older brother, Gary, was a good athlete, so I really had no choice but to give it my best. There were times when I thought Dad was pushing too hard, but he saw an ability in me for playing ball and encouraged me to stretch farther than I thought I could. I know I never would have enjoyed the success I've had as an athlete if it hadn't been for my dad. Our family was very close and remains so to this day.

My main sport was baseball until I was eight years old. Then I begged my dad to let me play football. He tried to talk me out of it, but I thought I knew best. He gave in and allowed me to try out.

After the first day of practice, I decided I didn't like football. I went to Dad and told him he was right and that I didn't need to play. He told me that he had paid $10 for me to play, and there was no way I was going to quit now.

I continued to play baseball, football, and basketball on into high school, but then I decided that my best shot at getting a college scholarship was in football. A lot of kids get burned out playing sports at such an early age, but I didn't.

I was drafted by the Chicago Cubs my senior year at Banks High School in Birmingham, but then I made my decision to choose the University of Alabama's Crimson Tide over the LSU Tigers. There were many reasons I chose Alabama. My dad had played there on a baseball scholarship and my brother on a football grant. I wanted a college education more than I wanted to play football. Alabama seemed the logical place to do both.

Coach Bear Bryant and several Alabama National Championships also helped me in my decision. Tuscaloosa was very close to my Birmingham home, so my family could come see me play.

My junior year we ended up number two in the country. Then my senior year in 1978, we won the national championship by beating Penn State in the Sugar Bowl. When I look back at my college career, my goal and our team goal was to win the national championship. I can always say we accomplished it. Besides that, playing Auburn every year was exciting too. I seemed to have my better games against Auburn, and I always looked forward to playing them.

I have fond memories of my days at Alabama. I really started to grow spiritually there by attending the Fellowship of Christian Athletes with my teammates Steadman Shealy and Keith Pugh.

I asked Jesus Christ to come into my life when I attended Vacation Bible School at church while I was eight years old. But it wasn't until I got into college that I really began any real spiritual growth. In college I started attending Bible studies and hanging around with other Christian friends. I think that is a key in any Christian's life: being careful who you spend your time with. Your friends will make you or break you! We must be accountable to someone, and that someone had better be a Christian who shares the same beliefs.

While in college, I also was involved with the Navigators, and I was really into their Topical Memory System where I was held accountable for memorizing Scripture that has stayed with me all of my life. I'm really thankful for that.

After graduating from Alabama, I was drafted in the ninth round by the Los Angeles Rams and then traded to the Giants in 1982. My pro career has been spent mostly being a backup quarterback. That has really been tough, especially when you know you have the qualifications of a starter, but you have to remember that you are where you are for a reason.

I work in every practice just as though I were preparing to start every game. When you are a backup at any position, you must be ready to go in and not let your team down.

In 1983 I came off the bench and had three, 300-yard passing games and victories as a starter. I had good games because I was ready. Then just as things were looking great for my career, I suffered a kneecap injury that cost me five weeks on the disabled list and my starting position.

Young people who want to be successful as an athlete must, first of all, develop solid work habits. If you don't have good habits in school and studying, you won't have good habits on the football field. I've seen players with a small amount of ability, but they possessed a willingness to work like crazy. These are the guys who make extra-special athletes. Remember, the best ability is availability: always work your hardest at everything you attempt, and you will be rewarded.

MIKE HAYNES, Defensive Back, Los Angeles Raiders, 6'2"—190 lbs. (PHOTO COURTESY OF LOS ANGELES RAIDERS)

15
Mike Haynes
Defensive Back
Los Angeles Raiders

"My leg was swollen like a balloon and covered with miles of bandages."

In 1976, I was drafted by the New England Patriots in the first round. I was the fifth player in the nation and the first defensive back to be picked in that draft, and I was named "Rookie of the Year."

I always considered myself a Christian. I was reared in church and attended regularly. My parents sent just us children at first, but as we grew older, they went with us. One Sunday morning when I was about fourteen, I boldly announced that I was not going to church anymore—I just didn't think it was necessary for a grown fellow like me. My mom was very unhappy with my decision, but after unsuccessfully pressuring me to change my mind, she decided not to force me to go.

Although not yet a Christian, I had always believed that God loved me and was somehow guiding my life. Several times in my youthful days, I got serious enough to pray, especially during a major decision or an important game.

I always prayed a lot and attributed my success in football as God's answer to my prayers. I remember an important playoff game with Oakland in 1976. I had hurt my right leg in a game against Tampa the week before. Actually, it was the calf muscle in my right leg. Our standing was eleven wins and three losses, and the outcome of this game was crucial. My leg was swollen like a balloon and covered with miles of bandages.

I was limping around, barely able to walk. In the locker room the coach asked me if I could play, and I said, "No way!" He sat me down and said, "Mike, you're tough. You're all-pro. You're too tough to let a little thing like a swollen leg keep you out of an important game." On and on he went.

I started walking around the locker room, and I looked at all the guys and saw how important the game was to them and how much they were hoping I could play. I went over to the corner by myself, and although I still had not asked Christ into my life, I said something like this to Him: "I promise, if You will help me play in this game, I'll do something for You with my life."

Well, it was a small miracle, but I played the entire game. Because of my regular attendance in Sunday School and church, I had heard hundreds of sermons and Bible lessons. I had been challenged to live a good, clean life. I admired men who stood up for Christ, and several of my teammates were committed to Jesus Christ.

I had attended some of our chapel services where I heard men of God who continued to influence my life. I also attended several weekly Bible studies conducted by a fellow Patriot, John Hannah, and some other team members. I knew these guys had something I didn't have. Their familyrelationships were great, and their experiences were different from what I had known. I had thought that making pro ball would be the ultimate experience. But I found out it wasn't.

Something was always missing in my life. Money and popularity just didn't satisfy me. I knew there had to be something else, and one Sunday morning I found the answer.

As I listened to the sermon, I was challenged to make sure that I was a Christian by inviting Christ into my life, and I knew that was what I really wanted to do. When the invitation was given, I asked Christ into my life and told Him that I was willing for Him to change and control me.

There was no immediate, dramatic change. I just knew that I was born again. But as I faithfully attended Bible studies with other Christians, I began to grow, and my life did a 360-degree turnaround. John Hannah shared what became my favorite Scripture found in the Book of Colossians (3:23-24): "Whatsoever ye do, do it heartily, as to the Lord, and not unto men; Knowing that of the Lord ye shall receive the reward of the inheritance: for ye serve the Lord Christ."

Through a series of growing events, I began to see my career in an entirely different light. Suddenly, I realized that I was playing football not to satisfy the coach or my teammates, nor to entertain the spectators and fans from Boston. Now, I believed that I was playing to glorify Christ, and daily I was in the process of becoming all that God had made and planned for me to be.

I didn't know where I was headed before, but I know that Christ came into my life at a time when I needed Him—a twenty-two-year-old guy, just out of college, with more money than I had ever dreamed of. I'm sure that He saved me from lots of problems. And as I learn and grow as a Christian, I have the feeling that I'm headed in the right direction. I feel that my life is just starting to take off.

During a meeting of Christian athletes held in Dallas, more than 100 professional players and their wives shared their faith in Christ as we fanned out across the metroplex. I was assigned to a boys' home in the area. While I shared Christ with them, eight guys prayed to receive Christ. This was one of the biggest thrills of my life.

I just hope that I might be an example to this younger generation. I have found it is not only the educational system that needs to be changed. The only way to change this society is to change the hearts of people *first*. Only God can do that.

STEVE FOLSOM, Tight End, Dallas Cowboys, 6'5"—240 lbs. (PHO-
TO COURTESY OF DALLAS COWBOYS)

16
Steve Folsom
Tight End
Dallas Cowboys

"I couldn't believe my shoulder pads were on backwards!"

My older brother, Scott, and I had a great time growing up together in Southern California. With all the broken homes there are now, I am very thankful Mom and Dad were always together and always supporting us in everything we attempted. Well, they supported us in everything we attempted if it was the right thing to do.

Downey, California, was near the beach, so we spent a lot of time there. Mom worked for a food company; Dad worked for the gas company. We were a typical middle-class family living in a typical middle-class neighborhood. The Mendozas across the street were our best friends. Their three sons were what kept Scott and me interested in athletics.

I was born in downtown Los Angeles, and we moved to Downey when I was five. Before we moved, I didn't care a thing about sports, but the Mendozas changed that forever.

I always attended church with my mom and dad and even went to a Catholic school until the sixth grade. In the seventh grade, I transferred to a public school because there was no basketball or any other sports at the Catholic school where my big sport was hopscotch!

My main game was basketball. I was very tall for my age and loved to play with the round ball. I made the basketball team as a freshman, so I naturally thought I had a great future on the hardwood court.

Then in the spring football season at the end of my freshman year, the football coach asked me to come out and play quarterback. I was excited about playing quarterback, but I should have known it wasn't for me. I was terrible! I couldn't throw the ball because the only way I knew how to throw was to pitch it like a baseball. To make matters even worse, my brother noticed when I came out of the dressing room my first day of practice that my shoulder pads were on backwards. Luckily, not too many guys noticed.

Thank goodness when the coach saw I was not quarterback material, he didn't give up on me. One day in practice he told me to try tight end, and that is where I have played ever since.

My main sport was still basketball, and I enjoyed it much more than football. Then in my senior year, I got several scholarship offers to play football. It wasn't until then that I realized I must be better in football than basketball.

I played in an All-Star game my senior year, and I was named the most valuable player. I guess that helped me get recognized by some colleges because I got several offers for scholarships.

I chose to accept a football scholarship at Long Beach State University because I really liked the coaches there. I played there one year, and my coaches moved to the University of Utah. So, I moved there with them. Man, is Utah different from Southern California!

I had a good career at Utah, and in my senior year I even got to play basketball. That year I played with two excellent players by the name of Tom Chambers and Danny Vranes. We went to the NCAA and eventually ended up tenth in the nation. What an experience for a football player!

I was drafted by the Miami Dolphins in the tenth round and was released during training camp. The Eagles picked me up halfway through the season. During training camp the next year, somebody left a tape in my locker by a guy named Josh McDowell. I threw the tape into my bag and left for home.

Later that night, I took the tape out and played it. What I heard made a lot of sense. This thing about having a personal relationship with the God of the universe sounded good. At the end of the tape, the speaker said all I had to do to have this relationship was to ask Jesus Christ to come into my life and take control. So, I did what he said and went to bed.

I continued to go to church and attend my team Bible studies and chapels, but it wasn't until 1985 that I realized what I had really done on my knees three years earlier. I was in the USFL, and it went outof business, so I had to sit out for a year doing nothing. During that time, I visited with a friend of mine in Laguna Beach, and after talking about the Lord and what He should mean in my life, I decided to rededicate my life to Jesus and follow Him in fullobedience with nothing held back.

I started taking my Bible study and prayer life seriously, and my spiritual life really starting coming together. It's amazing that when our spiritual lives are growing, the rest of our lives just seem to fall into the place right after the spiritual

I think kids now should participate in as many sports as they enjoy and not concentrate on any one sport until they are at least in high school.

Always remember that you can be no smarter on the field than you are in the classroom.

DONNIE SHELL, Former Strong Safety, Pittsburg Steelers, 5'11"—190 lbs. (COURTESY OF PITTSBURG STEELERS)

17
Donnie Shell
Strong Safety
Pittsburgh Steelers

"Coach told me that old cliche, 'Quitters never win, and winners never quit!' "

One of the fondest memories of my childhood was going to church with my family in a rural area of South Carolina. But, as I approached my pre-teen years, I noticed that my clothes were not like most of the other kids who attended Sunday School and church. Most of my clothes were coveralls, handed down from my older brother.

With nine children in my family, there just wasn't enough money in those days to buy each of us church clothes. I began to make excuses why I did not want to go to church, but the real reason was because I was ashamed of my clothes. I envied other boys who had shirts and pants.

As a teenager, however, I set a mature goal—to get a good education so I could make enough money to help my family. I was willing to make any sacrifice to attain my goal. But, an unfavorable report card in high school almost thwarted my plans. I was attending a school where my race was primarily in the minority, and the resistance to integration was at a high point. In one of my classes, all seemed to be going well, until I found out that I was the lone black student who failed the course. I really thought that I was being treated unfairly, and I determined that I would quit that school and enroll in a predominantly black school many miles from my home.

When I went to inform Coach William O. Johnson about my decision to transfer to an all-black school, he told me that I was all wrong for wanting to quit when things got tough. He said he believed that I was a good football prospect for a college scholarship if I stayed and did my best. Coach gave me that old cliche, "Quitters never win, and winners never quit." I knew he was right, and I decided to stick it out as long as I could. There was no possible way for me to attend college except through a sports scholarship. My parents certainly could not help me financially, and I would never be able to attain my educational goal without going to college.

After graduating from high school, and only a few weeks before the fall quarter was to begin, I got an athletic scholarship from South Carolina State. I thought that everything was finally going my way. But, before school started, another horrendous problem raised its ugly head.

Even though I worked as hard as I could, my SAT tests were low, and it looked as if I wouldn't be able to get into State. My Mother and I prayed as hard as we could, and the good Lord just made it possible for me to barely get in.

I thank the Lord that I have been able to complete a degree in physical education and a Master's degree in guidance and counseling before going into pro football.

In 1974, I signed with the Pittsburgh Steelers as a free agent and became a regular for the first time in 1977, winning a starting-free safety position in training camp and preseason games. When Mike Wagner suffered a neck injury and was side lined for a year, I moved to a strong safety and maintained that position for the last several years of my NFL career.

I really became a Christian in 1974 but commit ted my life entirely to Christ at a conference in 1978. I consider my born-again experience the highlight of my life, and I really enjoy living and witnessing for Christ.

God has allowed me to serve as chapel leader for the Pittsburgh Steelers, and we saw attendance grow to more than thirty players at various times.

I really enjoy sharing my faith with high-school and college athletes during Sports World Ministry every spring. We have seen hundreds of young players come to know Jesus Christ as their person al Savior during these sharing times. God has been so good to me. I love my family. I love football. I love life, and I believe that all of these wonderful

things happened to me because I love the Lord
Jesus Christ.

After an incredibly successful career, Donnie
Shell retired from the Steelers.

DENNIS HARRISON, Former Defensive End, Philadelphia Eagles, 6'8"—280 lbs. (PHOTO COURTESY OF VANDERBILT UNIVERSITY COMMODORES)

18
Dennis Harrison
Defensive End
Philadelphia Eagles

"We never *walked* off the practice field!"

Mom always taught us to do the best, no matter what we were doing. She not only told us this, she also did the best she could to enforce it.

Murfreesboro, Tennessee, is a good-sized town just southeast of Nashville. This is where Mom raised her ten children and gave them everything she had.

I started playing football at Bradley Elementary School in Murfreesboro when I was in the eighth grade. I played offensive and defensive line, the positions I played all the way through high school. The only reason I played football was to be with my friends.

During my freshman year, I had one of the toughest coaches of my life to this day: Bobby Modrell. He was a strict disciplinarian and would enforce rules such as not walking on or off the practice field. If you did, the whole team would run for your mistake. Little rules like this seemed awful trivial at the time, but later they helped me to be tougher than other players who played for easier coaches.

Another coach I had was Bill Blair. He was also very tough but always very fair. I figured if I could play for them, I could play for anybody.

I went to Murfreesboro Central High School my sophomore year; then our school was split into two schools, and I went to Riverdale High School. In my senior year I played defensive line and tight end. I think I played tight end because the quarterback couldn't see over me to throw the ball.

I was also on the wrestling team. I went undefeated my senior year and won the state championship. I was six feet, four inches, and weighed 240 pounds. I made All State and was named the MVP in the State All-Star game.

Steve Sloan was the coach at Vanderbilt University, and he really had turned a losing program into a winning team. I decided to accept a scholarship to play for the Commodores and stay close to home in Nashville. I also wanted to be part of a program that was building a new tradition. This was also true about Vandy, for in my freshman year we went to the 1974 Peach Bowl, and I was named the Most Valuable Defensive Player of the game.

In my junior year at Vanderbilt that I realized I might get to play pro football. These thoughts came true in my senior year as I was drafted in the third round by the Philadelphia Eagles.

While in the pros, I played in the Pro Bowl in 1982 and in the Super Bowl. We lost the Super Bowl, but it was still an incredible experience. Another accomplishment I am very proud of is the fact that I made it through Dick Vermeil's training camp. Man, was he tough! There again, I thought back to my freshman high-school year under Coach Modrell playing for the Bradley Eagles. The way he was tough on me then helped me to get through training camp with Coach Vermeil as a first-year pro.

The event that most affected my life and my football game happened during the summer of 1982. A year earlier, my wife had asked Jesus Christ to come into her life, and I could really see a change that I couldn't understand. We moved back to Nashville after living in Philadelphia for three years, and we started attending church at Lighthouse Baptist where our oldest child was in school.

After running out of excuses not to attend church with my family, I finally went. About my third Sunday, I realized that being a good person was not good enough to get me to heaven. That Sunday, when the pastor gave the invitation to walk the aisle and ask Christ to come into my life, I did it.

I didn't see any stars or fireworks go off as a result of my decision. It was kind of like eating and never being full before. Now I see how to get full.

My favorite Scripture verse is Romans 10:9 which says, "If thou shalt confess with thy mouth the Lord Jesus, and shalt believe in thine heart that God hath raised him from the dead, thou shalt be saved." I always had a head knowledge of God, but I had never taken that knowledge of Him into my heart.

Being a Christian freed me up to be the best football player I could possibly be, by taking the pressure off myself to excel to please other people. Now I played to the best of my ability to please Christ and Him only. Even when I had a bad game, I knew inside that if I had done my best, He was still pleased. And that makes all the difference in the world!

*After a highly productive career, Dennis Harrison recently retired from the Eagles.

JEFF SIEMON, Former Linebacker, Minnesota Vikings, 6'2"—237 lbs. (PHOTO COURTESY OF MINNESOTA VIKINGS, PHOTOGRAPHY BY BILLY ROBIN MCFARLAND)

19
Jeff Siemon
Linebacker
Minnesota Vikings

"Playing handball and basketball really help my agility in being a better football player."

When I got to college, I realized my whole world was made of plastic and was about to be crushed to pieces. Up until that time, I had never had a real confrontation with myself about the true meaning of life.

My dad was an eye doctor in Bakersfield, California, where I grew up. I graduated from Bakersfield High School where I excelled in athletics and academics. My father had instilled in me the idea that academics were more important than athletics.

I accepted a scholarship to play football for the Stanford Cardinals. In my freshman year, I suffered a knee injury that threatened to end my football career very abruptly. I began to wonder exactly what one could put one's faith in. What was that something that would bolster me and give me the peace of mind I needed when circumstances weren't perfect?

My roommate and I talked several times about what a relationship with Christ might be like. I had always attended church, but still something was missing. Finally, one night I told Jesus that I didn't know what in the world He had planned for me, but, I said, "I now ask You to come into my life and change it according to Your will".

Becoming a Christian didn't slow down my desire to excel, but, instead, it helped me to put it in a new perspective. I love to play, and I play to win. The desire to excel is as great in my mind as with anyone. I have heard it said that you can't be a winner if you lose graciously. I don't think that is true at all. I love to win, but being a Christian helps me not to be devastated when I lose.

While at Stanford, I was on the winning team of two Rose Bowls, and I was selected as an All-American my senior year at Stanford.

I was drafted by the Minnesota Vikings, and I have been fortunate to have been selected to play in the Pro Bowl five times. Every athlete needs to be realistic in evaluating his abilities. Assuming that you do have the ability, hard work, and determination necessary will keep you there.

Every summer, a lot of guys show up for training camp, and for the majority, the only thing that keeps them from making the team is *attitude*. They need that something extra inside that allows them to fully utilize their abilities. For me that something extra comes from a growing relationship with Jesus Christ.

From a practical point of view, the classical picture of a football player is the big, strong, aggressive hitter. It's true that hard hitting is a fact of life in football. But I've noticed the games that have increased my agility such as handball and basketball have helped me most to be a better linebacker.

I've been a starter for the Vikings every year since my rookie season, and I love the game. I take it seriously and never take for granted that just because I have been around awhile, I can coast. Every year gets a little tougher, and I can never stop learning more about my position.

Don't ever try to ride the fence and think you are impressing others by going along with them, while at the same time trying to maintain a strong Christian stand. Do what you know is right!

*After a stellar career, Jeff Siemon is now retired.

20
More Than Winning
Have You Discovered God's Plan for Your Life?

GOD'S PLAN

In most athletic contests a coach prepares a game plan ahead of time. God designed a plan for our lives before the world began. God is holy and perfect. He created us to love Him, glorify Him, and enjoy Him forever.

What Is God's Standard?

The Bible, God's playbook, says that the standard for being on His team is to:

Be holy.

"You shall be holy as I am holy"—1 Peter 1:16

Be perfect.

"Be perfect, therefore, as your heavenly Father is perfect"—Matthew 5:48

What Is God's Plan?

God created us to:

Love Him.

"Jesus replied: 'Love the Lord your God with all your heart and with all your soul and with all your mind' "—Matthew 22:37

Glorify (honor) Him.

"You are worthy, our Lord and God, to receive glory and

honor and power, for you created all things, and by your will they were created and have their being"—Revelation 4:11

Enjoy Him forever.

Jesus said, ". . . I have come that they may have life, and have it to the full—John 10:10

Why is it that we cannot live up to God's standard of holiness and perfection and fulfill God's plan for our lives? Because . . .

MAN'S PROBLEM

Man is sinful and is separated from God.

What Is Sin?

Sin means missing the mark, falling short of God's standard. It is not only doing wrong and failing to do what God wants (lying, gossip, losing our temper, lustful thoughts, etc.), but it is also an attitude of ignoring or rejecting God which is a result of our sinful nature. *"Surely I have been a sinner from birth, sinful from the time my mother conceived me"*—Psalm 51:5

Who Has Sinned?

"For all have sinned and fall short of the glory of God—Romans 3:23

What Are the Results of Sin?

Separation from God: *"But your iniquities* [sins] *have separated you from God . . . "*—Isaiah 59:2

Death: *"For the wages of sin is death . . . "*—Romans 6:23

Judgment: *"Just as man is destined to die once, and after that to face judgment"*—Hebrews 9:27

. . . God is holy and we are sinful and separated from him. Man continually tries to reach God through his own efforts (being good, religious activities, philosophy, etc.) but, while these can be good things, they all fall short of God's standard. *"All our righteous acts [good works] are like filthy rags"*—Isaiah 64:6

There is only one way to bridge this gap between God and man . . .

GOD'S SUBSTITUTE

God provided the only way to be on His team by sending His Son Jesus Christ as the holy and perfect substitute to die in our place.

Who Is Jesus Christ?

He is God.
Jesus said, *"I and the Father are one"*—John 10:30

He is Man.
" . . . the Word [Jesus] was God . . . The Word became flesh and lived for a while among us"—John 1:1,14

What Has Jesus Done?

He died as our substitute.
"God demonstrates his own love for us in this: While we were still sinners, Christ died for us"—Romans 5:8

He rose from the dead.
" . . . Christ died for our sins . . . he was buried . . . he was raised on the third day according to the Scriptures and . . . he appeared to Peter, and then to the Twelve. After that, he appeared to more than five hundred . . . "—(1 Corinthians 15:3-6)

He is the only way to God.
"I am the way, the truth, and the life. No one comes to the Father except through me"—John 14:6

. . . God has bridged the gap between Himself and man by sending Jesus Christ to die in our place as our substitute. Jesus defeated sin and death and rose from the grave. Yet,

it isn't enough to just know these facts. The following . . .
tells how to become part of God's team and experience His
plan . . .

MAN'S RESPONSE

Knowing a lot about a sport and "talking the game"
doesn't make you a member of a team. The same is true in
becoming a Christian. It takes more than just knowing
about Jesus Christ; it requires a total commitment by
faith in Him.

Faith Is Not:

Just knowing the facts.
*"You believe that there is one God. Good! Even the demons
believe that—and shudder"*—James 2:19
Just an emotional experience.
Raising your hands or repeating a prayer is not enough.

Faith Is:

Repenting. Turning to God from sin. *"Godly sorrow
brings repentance that leads to salvation and leaves no re-
gret . . ."*—2 Corinthians 7:10
Receiving Jesus Christ. Trusting in Christ alone for salvation. *"Yet to all who received him, to those who believed
in his name, he gave the right to become children of God . . .
"*—John 1:12,13
On which side do you see yourself?
Where would you like to be?

Jesus said, *"I tell you the truth whoever hears my word
and believes him who sent me has eternal life and will not
be condemned; he has crossed over from death to life."*—
John 5:24
The following is a replay of what this commitment of faith
in Jesus Christ is all about . . .

REPLAY OF GOD'S PLAN

Realize God is holy and perfect; we are sinners and cannot save ourselves.

Recognize who Jesus is and what he's done as our substitute.

Repent by turning to God from sin.

Receive Jesus Christ by **faith** as Savior and Lord.

"Yet to all who received him, to those who believed in his name, he gave the right to become children of God . . ."—John 1:12,13

Respond to Jesus Christ in a life of **obedience**.

". . . if anyone would come after me, he must deny himself and take up his cross daily and follow me"—Jesus, Luke 9:23

Does God's plan make sense to you? Are you willing to repent and receive Jesus Christ? If so, express to God your need for him. If you're not sure what to say, consider the "Suggested Prayer of Commitment" [that follows] . . . Remember that God is more concerned with your attitude than with the words you say.

Suggested Prayer of Commitment

"Lord Jesus, I need You. I realize I'm a sinner and I can't save myself. I need Your mercy. I believe that You died on the cross for my sins and rose from the dead. I repent of my sins and put my faith in You as Savior and Lord. Take control of my life and help me to follow You in obedience. In Jesus' name, Amen."

". . . if you confess with your mouth, 'Jesus is Lord,' and believe in your heart that God raised him from the dead, you will be saved . . . for 'everyone who calls on the name of the Lord will be saved' "—Romans 10:9,10,13

Once you have committed your life to Jesus Christ, it is

important to understand what your position is on His team . . .

KNOW YOUR POSITION

Too many people make the mistake of measuring the certainty of their salvation by their feelings instead of the facts of God's Word.

In Jesus Christ you have a new life. See what God's Word says about your new position on His team . . .

N I am a *New Creation* in Christ. 2 Corinthians 5:17; Galatians 2:20

E I have *Everything* I need for life and godliness. 2 Peter 1:3; Ephesians 1:3

W I am a *Witness* for Christ and am His *Workmanship*, created for good works. Acts 1:8; Ephesians 2:10

L I am *Loved* and accepted completely in Christ. Ephesians 1:6; Romans 8:39

I I am *Indwelt* by the Holy Spirit. 1 Corinthians 6:19,20; 1 John 4:4

F I am *Forgiven* and *Free* from condemnation. 1 John 1:9; Romans 8:1-2

E I have *Eternal Life* in Christ. John 5:24; 1 John 5:11-13

Trust God! Put your faith in His Word, not in your feelings. *"I write these things to you who believe in the name of the Son of God so that you may know that you have eternal life."—1 John 5:13*

SEVEN DAILY EXERCISES

Just as physical growth demands physical exercise, spiritual growth as a Christian demands spiritual exercise. To build spiritual muscle here are seven daily exercises:

1. Daily Die to Self.

". . . In Christ Jesus our Lord I die daily" (1 Corinthians

15:31). Yield complete control of your life to Jesus Christ every day.

2. Daily Obedience to Christ.

"Then he said to them all: If anyone would come after me, he must deny himself and take up his cross daily and follow me" (Luke 9:23). Every day commit yourself to obeying God and His Word.

3. Daily Bible Reading.

" . . . they examined the Scriptures every day" (Acts 17:11). Spend time every day reading God's Word. First read through the Gospel of John, one chapter per day.

4. Daily Prayer.

". . . give us this day our daily bread" (Matthew 6:11). Devote time every day talking to God in prayer.

5. Daily Fellowship.

"Encourage one another daily" (Hebrews 3:13). Get involved with your local church and seek regular fellowship with other Christians.

6. Daily Witnessing.

"Day after day . . . they never stopped teaching and proclaiming the good news that Jesus is the Christ" (Acts 5:42). Witness for Jesus Christ every day through your words and actions.

7. Daily Praise.

"Seven times a day will I praise Thee" (Psalm 119:164). Every day praise God for who He is and what He has done.

Do these exercises and you will grow strong in your Christian life and be an effective member of God's team.